Jane Goodall
A Little Golden Book® Biography

By Lori Haskins Houran

Illustrated by Margeaux Lucas

🐦 A GOLDEN BOOK • NEW YORK

Text copyright © 2024 by Lori Haskins Houran
Cover art and interior illustrations copyright © 2024 by Margeaux Lucas
All rights reserved. Published in the United States by Golden Books, an imprint of
Random House Children's Books, a division of Penguin Random House LLC, 1745 Broadway,
New York, NY 10019. Golden Books, A Golden Book, A Little Golden Book, the G colophon,
and the distinctive gold spine are registered trademarks of Penguin Random House LLC.
rhcbooks.com
Educators and librarians, for a variety of teaching tools, visit us at
RHTeachersLibrarians.com
Library of Congress Control Number: 2022949675
ISBN 978-0-593-64734-9 (trade) — ISBN 978-0-593-64735-6 (ebook)
Printed in the United States of America
10 9 8 7 6 5 4 3 2 1

Valerie Jane Morris-Goodall was born in London, England, on April 3, 1934. Her parents called her Jane.

When Jane turned one year old, her father gave her a toy chimp named Jubilee. Jane took Jubilee everywhere. She hugged and patted him so much he started to lose his fur!

Jane loved real animals, too. She spent hours
watching earthworms and sea snails. She taught
tricks to her dog, Rusty.

She even made friends with some robins who
visited her bedroom window.
They built a nest on Jane's bookshelf!

One of Jane's favorite books was *The Story of Doctor Dolittle*, about a man who could talk to animals. In the tale, Dolittle goes to Africa.

Jane made a decision. She would go to Africa, too, and study wild animals.

Jane was only eight years old, but she already knew exactly what she wanted to do with her life. There was just one question: How could she make it happen?

If things were different, Jane might have gone to college to be a scientist. But her family didn't have enough money for college, and there weren't many female scientists at the time. It didn't seem like a path Jane could pick. She became a secretary instead, filing papers in an office.

For a while, her dream felt very far away.

Then Jane got lucky. A friend moved to Kenya, Africa. Would Jane like to visit her?

YES, she would!

Jane saved up her money for months. At last, she had enough for boat fare to Africa. She arrived the day before she turned twenty-three.

Africa was spectacular. Jane saw wildlife everywhere.

On her trip, Jane met a scientist named Louis Leakey. She impressed him with her passion for animals.

Jane didn't know it, but Louis was looking for someone to study chimpanzees in Tanzania, Africa. He didn't want a trained scientist like himself. No, Louis wanted someone with fresh eyes. Someone patient, curious, and brave.

Someone just like Jane!

In July of 1960, Jane pitched a tent in Tanzania's Gombe forest. She unpacked her binoculars and her notebooks.

Jane's dream was coming true!

Gombe was beautiful but full of danger.
There were steep cliffs. Hungry leopards.
Stinging insects. Poisonous snakes.

Jane didn't worry much about those things.
She worried about something else—how to
find the chimpanzees. Where *were* they?

Jane tramped all over the forest, searching.
She hiked up hills and crawled through bushes.
Once in a while, she spotted some chimps.
The trouble was, they spotted her, too—and the
second they did, they ran away.

Jane didn't give up. She waited and waited.
Finally, one of the chimps began to trust her—
an old chimp that Jane named David Greybeard.
He let Jane get close enough to watch him.
And what Jane saw was incredible.

David pulled the leaves off a twig, then stuck it in a mound of dirt. When he pulled the twig back out, it was covered with insects. David gobbled them up.

Why was this so amazing? David had made the twig into a tool. Until that moment, scientists thought only humans could make tools. No one had ever seen an animal do it!

Jane shared her discovery with Louis Leakey.
He was stunned. So was the world.

"Now we must redefine man, redefine tool, or accept chimpanzees as humans!"

National Geographic magazine wanted pictures of the chimpanzees. They sent a photographer named Hugo van Lawick to Gombe.

Jane felt annoyed. She liked having the forest and the chimps to herself. Who was this Hugo? Would he bug her? What if he got in the way?

It turned out Hugo did not bug Jane. He was helpful, actually. And rather handsome.

Hugo took photo after photo of the chimps. He took photo after photo of Jane, too.

Jane and Hugo fell in love and got married. A few years later, they had a baby boy. They named him Hugo after his dad but called him Grub.

Meanwhile, Jane got to know more about the chimps in Gombe. She gave them all names: Flo, Fifi, Goliath, Mr. McGregor.

The chimps grew comfortable with her. Very comfortable!

Jane filled notebooks with records of the chimps' behavior. She wrote about how they hugged and kissed, laughed and cried, played and solved problems.

Her work showed that chimpanzees had feelings. They were smart, too. Chimps were a lot like humans.

Some scientists scoffed at Jane. They said she should give the chimps numbers, not names. And she shouldn't befriend them. That wasn't proper.

Jane scoffed right back. She was finding out more about chimpanzees—FAR more—than anyone else in the world.

Jane studied the Gombe chimpanzees for many years. Then, in 1986, Jane decided she needed to do more. She needed to help animals *everywhere*.

She circled the globe, urging people to protect the earth and its creatures. She started a program called Roots & Shoots, for kids who wanted to help.

"What you do makes a difference, and you have to decide what kind of difference you want to make," Jane said.

Jane traveled three hundred days a year. Still, she visited the chimps whenever she could. She stayed a part of their lives for more than sixty years.

From a young age, Jane knew just what she wanted—a life full of animals and adventures. And she got it!